Battle of the Mind

Nika Collins

Copyright © 2019 Nika Collins

All rights reserved. No part of this publication may be reproduced, distributed, or transmitted in any form or by any means, including photocopying, recording, or other electronic or mechanical methods, without the prior written permission of the publisher, except in the case of brief quotations embodied in critical reviews and certain other noncommercial uses permitted by copyright law.

ISBN-13: 978-1-951300-88-3

Liberation's Publishing LLC
West Point, Mississippi
www.liberationspublishing.com

Contents

Introduction 5

1 Childhood Trauma 7

2 Embracing Your Pain 13

3 Spiritual Warfare 17

4 The Healing Process 23

5 Recognizing Your Strengths 29

6 Living in The Present 33

7 Reprogramming Your Mind 37

8 Purpose 39

9 Beauty for Ashes 41

10 Finding Your Voice 49

11 Overcoming Fear 53

12 From Weakness to Strength 59

13 Guard Your Heart 65

Introduction

Some days the will to continue fighting this battle may feel impossible, there are countless circumstances that leave us feeling powerless. But in those very moments, what seems like a hindrance/threat to our lives may be the platform God uses for his Glory to be displayed through us. As we stumble along, we often wonder, where is God? Why is he allowing me to go through this? We feel stuck and broken. The reality is however, that God does his best work in our darkness and whatever journey God begins in your life and heart, he promises to finish- in his perfect timing. I wrote this book due to my own experiences with depression/anxiety.

God has been consistent in his guidance and has always been there to cover and protect me. Anxiety/Depression will not win! God promises us that in the end it will all be worth it, and we'll understand everything we went through along the way.

I hope this book will change your life forever.

This book is dedicated to my mother Lottie Campbell. My mom's love, compassion and strength has really been a blessing in my life. I'm forever grateful for her example. To my husband, the man of my dreams, my best friend, my shoulder to cry on. Malcolm Collins, I dedicate this book to you also. To my wonderful children, the love of my life, I couldn't imagine life without you. The Best Is Yet to Come!

1 Childhood Trauma

I wasn't the little girl who grew up with a silver spoon in her hand. It seemed as if my life was always difficult. As a little girl I remember always second guessing myself. When I entered a room, I wondered what people thought. I wondered if all the pain on the inside of me was showing up on the outside. A hidden fear of rejection always loomed over my head. Not having a father in my life made me feel incomplete. Seeing other kids with both parents was hard to watch, because it was what I longed for.

My mom raised us as a single parent. We were a church going family. Knowing the Lord was a must and mom made sure that we attended church rather we wanted to or not. She is the true definition of a Christian woman. Even so, I watched my mom struggle daily just to make sure that her children were ok. Sometimes she would even walk to work in freezing temperatures. We always had everything we needed, but not much else.

School was something I hated. I felt worthless. They say, "sticks and stones may break my bones, but words never hurt." That's not true. For the longest time, I heard the voice of the little boy that sat in the desk next to me. He was always so ugly towards me. I replayed him telling me that I would never be nothing; I was fat and ugly. For years I could still hear the laughs and giggles as I walked by. I didn't feel accepted by others. I felt empty.

My grades were low; I had no will power. I promised myself that when I grew up things would be different. My life would be different. I left home at the age of 18 with no plan at all. I started drinking, clubbing, and running the streets. I wanted to fill the emptiness that I felt in my soul. I didn't trust men, but I wanted to be loved. There were missing pieces in my life and one of the missing pieces was my father.

Fatherless-Daughter Syndrome is a disorder of the emotional system that leads to repeated dysfunctional relationship decisions, especially in the areas of trust and self-worth. Studies repeatedly show. That children without fathers positively present in the home suffer greatly. The psychological harm of father absence experienced during childhood persists throughout the life course. Non-resident fathers can have positive effects on children's emotional well-being. According to U.S. Census, "there is a "father factor" in nearly all of the societal ills facing America today."[1]

I've had difficulties interacting with men in all aspects of my life. I was never taught how to feel comfortable with a man, or I didn't know how to view a man. My esteem was low and settled for less so many times. I had pain, father hunger, and anger. So many times, I've wanted to yell and hug my father at the same time. I know that a father loss is a journey that will grow and change throughout my life.

I came to realize that I didn't want to continue feeling this loss that I felt from being fatherless. I'm embracing my emotions and believing that through it all I am growing in wisdom and re-silence. My brokenness has shown me strength that I

---

[1] https://cdn2.hubspot.net/hub/135704/file-396018955-pdf/RyanNFIFatherAbsenceInfoGraphic051614.pdf

never knew I had. I am who God says I am, and I refuse to allow my past to determine my future. Fearfully and Wonderfully Made. Psalm 139:14 reads, "I praise you because I am fearfully and wonderfully made; your works are wonderful." I know that full well.

Nika Collins

2 Embracing Your Pain

Why in the world would anyone want to embrace pain? And how could something like pain be good for us? Pain is gain. It's something that we must accept into our experiences. We all need healing for the pains that have already occurred. I wish for healing and happiness for everyone in the world. There are so many people dealing with unimaginable pain. Pain of the body, pain of the mind, and most of all pain of the heart.

Realize the gift that pain brings. One thing is unavoidable, joy and pain are part of life, but your good days can outweigh your bad. All things happen for a reason. You don't see it yet, but you will. There are no coincidences. Have faith that whatever the situation is, it is happening out of love. There's a certain amount of pain that you need to become who God has called you to be. The stronger the pain the bigger calling. Pain will inspire you to help others. It makes you relate to their pain. You can't have joy without pain. When you numb pain, you numb joy.

Once you're free from pain you embrace freedom and space. Your appreciation and gratitude expand. Life is more vibrant, richer, and wonderful. Pain is our biggest teacher, EMBRACE IT!! I felt the constant burn of going through the fire. I indulged in this state and felt some form of relief from acknowledging all the suffering. I had come to believe someone else was guilty of inflicting this suffering on me. I lay blame on others for my ill feelings and continued to bleed deeply inside. I realized I was fighting against myself by not accepting my pain. If I was able to accept the positive experiences in my life what would happen if we did the same for other emotions that came into my life. Sadness, pain, fear, anger, and loneliness are real emotions and they are a common part of life.

Once I began to surrender and embrace all of life and the lessons it dispensed for my spiritual growth, I stopped seeking to blame someone else. I learned that when I embraced my pain all while shining a light on it, I could clearly see the depth and darkness of it. I'm learning to embrace my journey by faith. God will not put more on me than I'm able to bear. I'm learning to move through the flow that life offers. I'm learning to cope. When I embraced my pain, suddenly it didn't become so painful.

Nika Collins

3 Spiritual Warfare

In 2017 mom suffered a stroke. We didn't know what the outcome would be. We had never seen our mom sick in our life. She was always so happy, active, and healthy. She loved working and spending time with family; she was the life of the family. Nevertheless, mom was hospitalized for 15 days. During that time, she was given so many fluids and different medications while test after test was ran.

She continued to grow worse despite their efforts. Her blood pressure continued to creep up. The doctors were doing all that they could do. I refused to believe that my mom wouldn't make it out of that hospital. I know the type of God that I serve can and will work miracles. We serve a supernatural God and he is not limited to the laws of nature. He can do what human beings cannot do. He can make a way in our lives where it looks as if there's no way.

That's what we prayed that he would do in mom's life. We kept praying and oiling mom from head to toe while speaking life over her. I would lay on the hospital couch right next to her all night in constant prayer. I had faith that God would work it all out in his timing. God is a miracle working God.

We can speak God's word in our everyday lives. I would open the bible to Psalms 91 where God promises that he will give his angels charge over us and that no evil would come near us. I would read this scripture to her daily. One night while sleeping next to her, I was awakened at two o'clock in the morning. My thoughts were racing, my palms were sweaty. I had shortness of breath and fear.

Fear of the unknown, worry, and stress. That was my very first experience with this crippling illness. As the enemy attacked, I continued to pray. I asked the Holy Spirit to continue to surround the room with divine protection. I asked the lord to empower us against the lies and to grant us both strength and peace.

Praying can and will calm an anxious mind and fill your heart with peace. Do not be anxious about anything, but in everything by prayer with thanksgiving present your request to God. When anxious thoughts, fear, panic, or worry try to come against you, present your request to God. It's very hard to bear the weight of anxiety and panic, you can't do it alone, so pray against the active enemy. God is with you always.

Prayer for anxiety is a very powerful thing. Learning to pray can calm an anxious mind and fill your heart with peace. Our Spiritual battles are real. To understand the battle of Spiritual Warfare, we need to begin with acknowledging that we are in a war. Battles make up smaller components of the bigger picture.

As Christians we are in a spiritual battle of some sort daily. Our spiritual battles and warfare are real even though we cannot physically see the attacker. Jesus told us to pray for God's will to be done on earth as it is in heaven. He tells us that the gates of hell will not prevail against the work that he has purposed for us. We will accomplish his will for our lives.

We will hit opposition but need to understand that the battle is not against flesh and blood but against powers in the heavenly places. As we begin to get a revelation of the spiritual warfare, we will begin to understand how the enemy moves against us in the physical realm.

Job was a real human living here on earth. He is a great example of a spiritual conflict that was manifested in the physical form. God looked upon Job as a righteous man, but because Satan wanted to prove God wrong, Job became the victim of Satan's attacks.

Job experienced very real physical and circumstantial conflicts because of the conflict in the spiritual realm. Job also became the victor because of his faithfulness to God in words and actions throughout his trials. After all the prayers and faith, God allowed mother to be released from the hospital. She still has a way to go but she's still here. God is a miracle worker if you only be still and allow him to work in all circumstances.

Nika Collins

4 The Healing Process

I was diagnosed with anxiety in 2017 but only recently decided to seek out a therapist. I refused to allow it to control my life. I decided to see a therapist. My decision to see a therapist was not an admission to lack of faith in God. It was faith that led me to reach out to someone to talk to. Mental health issues happen to everyday people, even to believers who are strong in faith.

For years I thought that going to see a therapist would be insane. I didn't want to be ostracized or appear weak, so I kept quiet and prayed that it would just go away. It didn't. I know now that God wants to heal me not shame me.

Emotional Trauma is very real. I was in the happiest chapters of my life. I was saved, happily married with four children, all coming from a single parent home. I defied the odds. Suddenly I started having debilitating panic attacks and didn't know why. Through therapy I learned that because I was grownup and safe all those painful events that I had experienced as a child began to surface. It was not because I didn't have faith. God loved me and knew it was time for me to heal from the pain of my past.

A soldier never experiences trauma when they're brave and fighting on the battlefield. They experience the pain when they're finally home. When they are safe to face what was too difficult to process at the time. Emotional Abuse has the same impact as Physical Abuse. You need to heal; you need to heal from PTSD. You're healing parts of your heart that you've once put to the side, whether to survive, to be strong, to avoid pain, or to take care of others.

This may be the most powerful act of faith that God is calling you to make today. The church is slow to address the realities of mental health. It's up to you as a regular, everyday person in the trenches of real life to speak the truth and tell our stories about the work God's doing in your life.

If you've been hurt, physically or mentally, you deserve to take care of yourself. Now that you're safe to heal with Jesus. God's word will give you strength to heal. Just like God used skilled doctors to help us heal from physical wounds, God uses psychologists to help heal our nervous system and process memories that once wounded us. We are free to sleep, rest and access all parts of our hearts. Many Christians may find it hard to confess that they are emotionally wounded. They may fear their faith being questioned.

Many pastors have committed suicide because they failed to seek help. They feared that other Christians believe anxiety was a sign of spiritual failure. Anxiety causes tremendous suffering to those who are afflicted. If you believe that a person is dealing with an anxiety disorder, please encourage them to get help.

Once person encouraging them in that direction may be all they need. Medications cannot cure anxiety disorders, but they may relieve a person's symptoms enough to help them to function and respond to psychotherapy. Anxiety is much more than a nervousness. The feelings of fear and anxiety that accompany them can be debilitating. The good news is that help is available, and these conditions can be managed with medical help and spiritual support.

To heal you must pass through the doorway of grief. Emotional wounds are beyond sadness. They're felt in the depth of your being. Honor your pain. Don't run from it. Give yourself permission to grieve. You will have some people push you to "Get over it". Ignore them. Time and patience are key to recovery. Surround yourself with friends who understand that.

I remember my first session of therapy as I opened up to my therapist. I couldn't find words. I struggled to swallow my grief and choked on my tears. But then, I let the tears flow. I cried long and hard gasping for air. I've always tried to dodge pain and heartache, but like everyone, it eventually found me. Deep pain always brings out the personal demons, such as blaming yourself, embracing victimhood, or, bitterness.

Whatever brings you peace of mind,

instead of longing for a miracle, create one. Use your pain to propel you in a new direction. It's been a tough couple of years, but I can honestly say that I'm fighting for my happiness but sometimes suffer with anxiety. It's not me all the time and it does not define me. I'm in my healing process.

5 Recognizing Your Strengths

What are your strengths? This is one of the questions that my therapist asked me. To be honest I couldn't answer the question. It was at that moment that I realized I didn't know what my strengths were. I felt so empty. I had no goals. I had no clue what I wanted to do with my life. There was no purpose.

When you see reflections of yourself through the eyes of those who know, you begin to identify your most unique talents. When it comes to accessing your talents, you are full of blind spots. If you start to see yourself through the eyes of others, your vision becomes clearer. We often look to others for qualities we want to develop within ourselves. We often forget that we're born with our own set of natural strengths that are just waiting to get out.

Identifying your own natural strengths and talents isn't always easy. It is well-worth your time to develop them. I've realized that one of my strengths is encouraging others. Despair and Anxiety have been an intrinsic part of life on earth. In times of darkness, Christians have sought the encouraging words of scripture to provide strength, wisdom, and guidance about the love and truth of God.

Words can tear down a person or they can also give life. I pray that my words will always be beneficial to those who hear them and be an encouragement to them. Ecclesiastes 4:9-12 declares that two are better than one, because they have a good reward for the toil. For if they fall, one will lift his fellow. But woe to him who falls and have not another to pick him up! Again, if two lye together, they keep warm alone. And though a man might prevail against one who is alone, two will withstand him-a threefold cord is not quickly broken. The mouth of the righteous is a fountain of life.

Life is full of problems, and we need to deal with them. But if we aren't careful, all we see are the problems. There are lots of good things we can focus on. Instead of catching people being bad, catch them being good. Make your words a fountain of life. Be a positive person. Encourage one another. Your greatest strengths reveal that they're tasks or actions that you can do well. Know Your Strength!

Nika Collins

6 Living in The Present

Choosing to live in the past robs you of the joy of today. The only important moment is the present moment. Stop living your life in the past and start living in the present. Fully appreciate the moment of today. Forgive past hurts. If you're holding grudges toward another person because of past hurts, choose to forgive and move on.

You cannot fully appreciate today if you're constantly worried about tomorrow. Tomorrow will happen whether of you worry about it or not. Bitterness and past hurts hold you hostage. They keep you from living a completely free life today.

I never thought that my past hurts, pains, and rejections would haunt me well into my adult life. Thanks to God I'm learning how to release the past for it is gone.

Live in the present and make it beautiful. Living in the present is crucial to success and being in the here and now. Seize every second of your life and savor it. Being present minded is the key to staying healthy and happy. It helps you fight anxiety, cuts down on your worrying and rumination by helping you take one moment and one day at a time.

Being present helps you deal with pain more effectively, reduce or stress, and decrease its impact on our health, while improve our ability to cope with negative emotions like fear and anger. Mistakes often linger in our mind and heart. Events from yesterday shift into our present day, never allowing us the freedom to fully move forward. Living under the weight of the "should haves" is a heavy burden to carry.

Sometimes the hardest person to forgive is the one staring back at you in the mirror. Shame, Rejection, Anxious, Depressed, Sick, Weak, Addicted, Adulterous, Lonely, Failure, Mistakes, Defeated, Confused, Broken and Hopeless. Even though we believe that Jesus has set us free, some labels are still written in what seems like permanent ink. It's a past not easily washed away by a good thought or an encouraging word.

The mind is a door that opens and closes. The enemy sometimes whispers sweet lies down deep inside our souls. Remember who you are. Remember where you've come from. Remember what you've done. You'll never change. The devil will often remind us of our failures and negative labels. The labels and mistakes of our past do not determine the reality of your future. Remember who you are in God. You've been forgiven and God wants you to live in your present.

7 Reprogramming Your Mind

I've always been one to worry about everything. I looked for the worst in every situation. I've always second guessed myself. I didn't open to anyone easily because of past hurts. I kept my guards up. Since therapy I'm learning to cope. I've learned that I do have control over my actions, thoughts, and feelings.

When I feel myself starting to go down a negative path, I become present and delete that bad thought. I'm learning that it's best to wipe the negative out. The enemy never plays fair. He will play with your mind if you allow him to. RESIST THE DEVIL AND HE WILL FLEE. All these things can be strongholds in your mind. There are days that the enemy will try to trick you. There are times when he will convince you that no one cares.

One day you're strong, but the next, you might spend it crying out for help. Satan has set out on a vicious mission to deceive us. Many times, the brilliant ideas and wonderful thoughts that come across my mind may seem so real and necessary, but they are all crippling tricks from the enemy. They are sent to hinder you on your walk with God.

One of the biggest tricks the enemy uses, is speaking to your mind, convincing you that you're not good enough, you're useless. Regardless of Satan's tricks and schemes, our God is a God of love and happiness. He never operates in confusion or deceit. The bible writes that the Thief cometh not, but for to steal, and to kill, and to destroy, I have come that they may have life, and that they might have it more abundantly.

8 Purpose

We all have purpose. It is during those tough times that we find out what we're really made of. God uses those test that we go through in life to refine us. He is shaping you into the person he wants you to be. Many times, I've questioned God when going through trials that I didn't understand. I've often asked God what is your purpose in this?

I've learned that in my struggles of life God is more interested in changing me than he is in changing my circumstances. Often, I've asked the question, God why am I here? What is my purpose? Everyone has a God-given purpose. We all have gifts, but we must use them for them to grow. Everyone has a talent. It's up to you to use it. Pray and ask God to show you the thing that moves you. He wants you to discover his purpose for you more than you do.

Your purpose is not just about you. It's about what God wants to do through you. God has called you to a purpose and wants you to walk in it. Jeremiah 29:11 is one of my favorite scriptures, For I know the plans I have for you, declares the Lord, plans to prosper you and not to harm you, plans to give you hope and a future.

We are all here for a reason. You must find what it is that makes you happy and energized. You might figure it out at the most unexpected moment. Your gift is very simple to know. Discover your gift and live in PURPOSE.

9 Beauty for Ashes

God why am I going through this? If God is good, why am I going through this? If God is good, why is this happening to me? If God is good, why am I struggling in this area? How many times have you asked God these questions?

God is good and he will give you beauty for your ashes. Establish your life on the word of God. Give God your ashes; give him your hurt; give him your pain; give him your bitterness; give him your past trauma.

God can renew your mind only if you allow him to. Walk in the blessings that God has prepared for you. Look forward to what God has spoken over your life. The ashes of life sometimes cause you to lose focus. But there is a season of beauty for you, and God is desiring to give you beauty for your ashes.

Sometimes it can be hard to reconcile the things that we go through. God's truth cannot be consumed by the trials of life. Once I was married to my husband in 2013, I thought for sure that now my life was complete. I was blessed with a beautiful family. What more could I ask for.

As a little girl, I always said that once I became an adult, I would do things different from what I saw growing up. I thought that I could prevent disappointment from showing its ugly head in my life. I Had dealt with enough, growing up! I had many unresolved problems that were left imbedded deep in my soul from childhood. I had so much anger and bitterness that I had carried over into my future.

Therapy and Prayer have become two of the most important things in my life. Emotional wounds are very real, but God is able and ready to renew your mind. I needed healing in my soul and didn't even know it. Many of my thoughts had been dark and lonely even in marriage.

My emotions were a mess. All that baggage of hurt was destroying my future. Isaiah 61:3 says, To console those who mourn in Zion, to give them beauty for ashes, the oil of joy for mourning, the garment of praise for the spirit of heaviness that they may be called trees of righteousness, the planting of the Lord, that he may be glorified.

Unless you give him your ashes you will not receive the beauty. If you hold on to them, he cannot give you beauty. What are your ashes? Wounds are your ashes, and everyone has ashes, and all kinds of them. Everybody gets wounded.

Oh, how I longed for beauty. Only when I let go and let God did things began to change. I still struggle at times, but it is amazing what God's grace will do in your life if you'll just press past the pain. Everything that I have been through has made me the strong woman that I have become today. The beauty of God's grace and mercy is amazing.

Many times, we become selfish when things do not turn out the way we want them to. Forgetting the many times God has kept us. God has come to rescue you. He wants to give you back your smile and give you beauty for your ashes. Life is not always happy. Sometimes it hurts. Sometimes it's hard. Sometimes it's dark and it leaves ashes where only God can find them.

These are the ashes felt from being deeply wounded. They are from being in a hard situation wondering if you'd ever come out. These ashes are from the loss of a loved one. They are from fear of the unknown.

Where was God in it all? Where is he now? His word declares that he was there during it all. Though we may not always see it, we can know beyond a doubt that he is with us. He will never leave us nor forsake us. John 16:33 says, in this world you will have trouble, but take courage, for I have overcame the world.

God is with you in whatever you may be facing. He is at work right now trading your ashes for greater beauty. God heals and the ashes of brokenness will fall away. His mercy brings beauty. So many times, we all have had to walk through the fire of hard situations and wondered if we would ever come out. God can bring you into complete restoration.

Just like many others I have laid awake in bed at night with racing thoughts and fear, fear of the unknown. It's not going to always be easy. Job was there too. This righteous man who loved and honored God. Yet he lost everything. And he knew without God he was nothing. Job sat in the ashes.

How could Job ask, "Though You Slay Me, Yet Will I Trust You." Job lost all his children, his wealth and health, but Job still trusted God. Job realized the suffering that he was enduring was allowed by God. Even in his pain he knew that God still had power over life and death. Nothing can shake the faith of someone who is grounded in the glory of God. Sometimes we may not understand what is happening or why, but just know that God is good, loving, and trustworthy. With God there is a way of escape. After this life there is eternal life with God in heaven if you only believe. God wants to give you beauty for the ashes.

Nika Collins

10 Finding Your Voice

A lot of times when we are really shaken, we stop talking. We become silent. I married at a very early age. The marriage was a complete failure! As we were going through a divorce, I realized that I needed to find out who I was. I needed to know who Nika really was! I needed to get back to self and loving me.

Once I did God sent me an amazing husband. The husband I have now is able to show me so many different things about myself. It is really teaching me how to move into a place of healing. It's very important to give voice to your pain. There are so many emotional struggles in life. We neglect to tell our story and how we were able to heal. Your voice is very important. Someone may need your voice to make it through something they're struggling with.

We all have a voice that needs to be used. Your voice makes a difference. For years I didn't know I had a voice. I didn't think that my voice mattered. Everyone has their own unique voice. Your voice could be the voice that changes a person's mind about contemplating suicide! You could literally save a person's life through your voice.

Rather it be a voice in writing, a voice behind the pulpit, or a voice on stage. My writing voice carries my experiences and personality. Your voice should reflect you. What you feel and believe, what moves you. Your voice counts. Someone may be in a dark place; they may be in that same dark season of their life that you just came out of. Your voice could be that voice that pulls them through that dark season of depression, low self-esteem, anxiety or whatever their illness may be. If you are in a season of pain, rest in God's word, remember his promises, he can heal your brokenness. There's no sorrow that Jesus can't heal. Many of us know what it's like to be emotionally hurt by friends, family, or even a spouse. We know what it's like to live with chronic pain or an illness that won't go away. A healing only God can give. Matthew 11:28-29 says, come to me, all of you who are weary and carry heavy burdens, and I will give you rest. Take my yoke upon you. Let me teach you, because I am humble and gentle at heart, and you will find rest for your souls. Proverbs 3:5-8 says, Trust in the Lord with all your heart, do not depend on your own understanding. Seek his will in all you do, and he will show you which path to take. Don't be impressed with your own wisdom. Instead, fear the Lord and turn away from evil. Then you will have healing for your body and strength for your bones. Speak up and declare Truth over your life. Declare the word of God. Sing it, pray it, write it down, and remind yourself what God says. Today be encouraged that you already have a voice and it is key in releasing life and hope right where you are.

11 Overcoming Fear

I have overcome so many things these last few days. Fear is one of the enemy's most popular weapons that he uses against us. Worry, anxiety, and fear can overwhelm us. We fear for our children's future. We fear so many different things. I've struggled with fear and worry for years. I found that relying on God's word often calms my thoughts.

Isaiah 41:10 tells us, do not fear, for I am with you, do not be dismayed, for I am your God. I will strengthen you and help you, I will uphold you with my righteous right hand. There is power in God's word. It gives power to our day. The physical feelings of fear can be scary in themselves, especially if you're experiencing them and don't know why.

There are mental and physical ways of tackling fear. Faith is key. Strong faith can provide a strong way of coping with everyday stress. In 2018 I was informed by my doctor that I had a large fibroid tumor that was the size a twenty-seven-week pregnancy. This shocking news triggered my anxiety. I was overwhelmed with fear. I worried about my finances because I knew that my recovery time would be six weeks.

I worried that the fibroid could be cancerous. I worried about the surgery itself. Once the surgery was completed. I wondered why I even spent all that time worrying about a procedure that went so smoothly. The fibroid tumor was benign (noncancerous). I didn't have any complications, and the whole six weeks that recovered the bills were still paid. I healed quickly with no complications.

All the fear and worry were for nothing. How many times have you become fearful about something? Putting faith in God means we believe, no matter how bad things look, that God will work them together for good. (Romans 8:28) When God says he will work all things for good, there is no exception.

Too often we look at what we are experiencing and cannot fathom how it will work out, but that's exactly when we need to place that situation into our father's capable hands. They are the very hands that created the world and we can rest, knowing that he has things under control. There are times in our lives when the road ahead seems uncertain. If we depend on our own understanding and reasoning, our faith will waiver.

My thoughts are completely different

from yours, says the lord. And my ways are far from beyond anything you could imagine. My ways are higher than your thoughts. There will be times when our faith in God requires us to believe in the impossible. All God wants is for us to stand still and know who He is. We can't continue trying to fight battles that are not ours to fight.

We must lean and depend on him and he will carry us through. God has all power and we are nothing without him. Having faith is so important. Faith goes beyond hope. Hope lives in the mind. Faith is deep-rooted in the heart and spirit. Faith is just as important as the air we breathe. Going through life and all its ups and downs can take a toll on us. But through all the trials and tribulations we might face, it's faith that gives us that helping hand. It guides us in the right direction, allowing us to discover our purpose in life.

Everything in life is far easier to get through when we have faith. Faith is simply trust. When your spirit, soul, and mind are full of bitterness, unforgiveness and resentment we cannot grow spiritually. Press pass anger and unforgiveness. Sometimes we don't feel strong within ourselves, on the other side of fear is your greatest destiny. Operate with courage because God is with you. You don't have to operate in your own strength. God will uphold you with his right hand.

So many times, I find myself questioning God asking, Father why am I going through this? Why is my life so hard? I'm trying to live for you but every time I try to take a step forward, I get knocked two steps backwards! But now I'm beginning to see that if God had not put me in all these uncomfortable situations I would've never pushed. I would have never known how strong I really am. In the end you will receive the fruits of your labor if you'll just stay in the fight.

12 From Weakness to Strength

You must walk through the low places of the process before you're equipped to live the promise. God had to take me through the process of getting unstuck from what's been holding me captive before I could take a stand. I had to keep walking the tightrope. One foot in front of the other. I had to catch my breath when needed while continuing to move forward.

You're not alone on your tightrope journey. Consider it pure joy my brothers and sisters, whenever you face trials of many kind, because you know that the testing of your faith produces perseverance. Finish its work so that you may be mature and complete, not lacking anything. James 1:2-4 Suffering will end. He will make us strong in the midst of our feeling weak. And there's a perfecting of us that's happening in the process.

God isn't far off he's just not interested in your being comfortable. God will take every cry you've uttered and arrange those sounds into a glorious song. So many times, I felt as if God had forgotten about me, maybe even abandoned me. I must confess there are times I get tired of hoping, weary from waiting, and I wander just how much longer it will all go on.

Through it all I thank God for reminding me that there is purpose to this process and I'm not walking through any of this alone. You are my strength. You are my hope. You are my song. Help me fix my eyes once again on your promises. Remind me to keep my hope tied to you and you alone.

For some of you this book will be exactly what you need to walk through a hard season or process a deep disappointment. For the last three years I've gone through so much warfare, but I know that he's expanding my testimony and increasing my faith.

In 2016 I was severely anemic and had to be rushed in for an emergency blood transfusion. In 2017 my mom had a massive stroke, and a few months later I was diagnosed with Anxiety. The following year 2018 I was told by my obstetrician that I had a huge tumor and it needed to be removed quickly. This year my son was diagnosed with myocarditis (inflammation of the heart).

The devil was attacking in so many different areas of my life, I started to become overwhelmed, anxious and fearful. The devil tried to attack my mind. I began to question God. I was reminded of Job and all he went through, yet trusted God. Job lost his money, his family and his health, but he remained strong to God. When Jesus hung on the cross, he suffered one of the worst deaths imaginable. He took on all the sins of humanity. Despite his innocence, he died for our sins.

The bible makes no promise to take away our suffering in this life. It does give us hope that suffering will one day be ended forever. Suffering can sweeten and deepen us. Suffering can poison and embitter us. We have a choice. As powerful as suffering is, God is more powerful. As real as suffering is, God is more real. As deep as suffering goes, God goes deeper. God is our refuge and strength, an ever-present help in trouble. Our weakness doesn't matter at all when we know where to find strength. God's grace is sufficient, and his power is made perfect in our weakness. Therefore, I will boast all the more gladly in my weaknesses, so that the power of Christ may rest on me.

Nika Collins

13 Guard Your Heart

How many times have you questioned God? How many times have you felt that God had abandoned you? We all have to go through adversity at some point in lives. Adversity is necessary. Many times, we won't grow until we're put under pressure. When things are adverse don't panic. Use those moments to grow.

So many times, I've felt as if my life was spiraling out of control. So many times, I wanted to give in, but I've learned that it's the struggles that has molded me into the woman that I have become, flaws and all. It was the struggle that pushed me. It was my test that has given me the testimony that I'm sharing with you today.

Did you know that every test is temporary? God promised that nothing is forever, everything is only for a season. In this season I'm discovering that we were all born with a gift. Being raised in a single parent home. Born in poverty. I was blinded to my gifts. I didn't believe in myself. Thanks to the Almighty God I am beginning to write a new chapter in my life. I am beginning to believe that I am who God says I am. I am the head and not the tail; I am above and not beneath. My future is in the gift that God gave me.

Retrain your mindset, discover your gift, dig deep if you have to. (Proverbs 18:16- A man's gift makes room for him and brings him before great men. Time is short, so we must wisely use the time that remains and shine the light of the gospel into the lives of those whom Satan has blinded. In this season I'm stepping into my purpose. I haven't laughed my best laugh, I haven't song my best song, I haven't thought my greatest thought, I haven't written down my greatest idea, I haven't dreamed my best dream, I haven't had my greatest day yet. My season is shifting. Jesus came so that we may have abundant life. Guard your heart and mind, you cannot continue listening to the accusing voice of the enemy. We have to stay focused God's promises. One of the tactics that the enemy uses against us is Fear. Fear is designed to send us in the opposite direction of God's will for our lives. 2 Timothy 1: 7-For God has not given us a spirit of fear, but of power and of love and of a sound mind. On the other side of fear is your greatest destiny.

What thoughts have entered into your heart and are now weighing you down? When your spirit, soul and mind get full of bitterness, unforgiveness and resentment you cannot grow spiritually. Press pass anger and unforgiveness. Operate in Love because God is with you. He will uphold you with his right hand.

Psalms 40 I waited patiently for the lord; and he inclined unto me and heard my cry. He brought me up also out of a horrible pit, out of the miry clay, and set my feet upon a rock, and established my goings. And he has put a new song in my mouth, even praise unto our God: many shall see it, and fear, and shall trust in the Lord. Blessed is that man that maketh the Lord his trust, and respecteth not the proud, nor such as turn aside to lies. Many, O Lord my God, are thy wonderful works which thou has done, and thy thoughts which are to us-ward: they cannot be reckoned up in order unto thee: if I would declare and speak of them, they are more than can be numbered. Sacrifice and offering thou didst not desire; mine ears hast thou opened: burnt offering and sin offering has thou not required. Then said I, Lo, I, come: in the volume of the book is written of me. I delight to do thy will, O my God: yea, thy law is within my heart.

Finally, be strong in the Lord and in his mighty power. Put on the full armor of God so that you can take your stand against the devil's schemes. For our struggle is not against flesh and blood, but against the rulers, against the authorities, against the powers of this dark world and against the spiritual forces of evil in the heavenly realms.

Therefore, put on the full armor of God, so that when the day of evil comes, you may be able to stand your ground, and after you have done everything to stand. Stand firm then, with the belt of truth buckled around your waist, with the breastplate of righteousness in place, and with your feet fitted with the readiness that comes from the gospel of peace. In addition to all this, take up the shield of faith, with which you can extinguish all the flaming arrows of the evil one. Take the helmet of salvation and the sword of the Spirit, which is the word of God. (Eph. 6:10-17)

Battle of the Mind

Nika Collins